CW01429251

Original title:

Unfurling Dreams Among the Fae Holt

Author: Sara Säde

ISBN HARDBACK: 978-1-80559-380-5

ISBN PAPERBACK: 978-1-80559-879-4

## A Serenade for the Enchanted

In twilight's hush, the stars do sing,
A dance of light on whispers' wing.
The moon's soft glow, it guides the way,
To realms where dreams and shadows play.

The breeze it carries tales of old,
Of love enchanted, brave and bold.
Each note a promise, soft and sweet,
Where time and magic gently meet.

### Reverie of the Woodland Spirits

Among the trees, the spirits twirl,
In golden leaves, their laughter swirls.
Their playful dance in silence flows,
As nature's heart in stillness knows.

The brook hums softly, secrets shared,
With mossy paths where few have dared.
In twilight's glow, their faces gleam,
Awakening the forest's dream.

## Blossoms of Fantasy and Light

Petals unfurl in joyful flight,
To greet the dawn with pure delight.
In every hue, a story glows,
Of wishes made and hope that grows.

Each fragrant breath, a spell is cast,
As magic melds with moments past.
In gardens where the fairies play,
The heart finds peace in bright array.

## The Veil of Hidden Whimsy

Behind the veil of shadows' play,
Whimsy dances, come what may.
With laughter light as morning dew,
It weaves a world both strange and new.

In secret corners, dreams unfold,
Where tales of wonder dare be told.
The spark of joy in every breath,
Defies the shadowed dance of death.

## Murmuring Memories of Winged Kin

In twilight's glow, the shadows sway,
Whispers of wings share tales of play.
Rustling leaves hold secrets dear,
Echoes of laughter, crystal clear.

A nest of dreams on branches high,
Songs of freedom fill the sky.
Soft feathers brush against the night,
Murmurs of kin take graceful flight.

Through blooming fields where wildflowers grow,
The dance of sparrows in the ebb and flow.
A lingering glance, a fleeting sigh,
Moments like clouds in the vast blue dry.

Each flutter tells of journeys past,
Boundless hopes that ever last.
In whispered winds, their stories weave,
A tapestry of those who believe.

As dusk descends, the chorus swells,
In every heart, a memory dwells.
Murmurs of kin, forever near,
In twilight's embrace, we hold them dear.

# Flickers of Fantasy in Murmuring Rivers

Beneath the stars, where waters gleam,
Flickers dance like a waking dream.
Whispers of currents, a playful tease,
Secrets flow on the gentle breeze.

In silver pools, reflections sigh,
Rippling tales of a moonlit sky.
With every ripple, a story told,
Of magical realms where hearts grow bold.

A boat drifts softly on tranquil waves,
Carving through paths where freedom braves.
Glimmers of hope shimmer and sway,
In murmuring rivers, where wishes play.

Time bends here in this sacred place,
Every glance a moment's grace.
Flickers of light guide the way,
In dreams' embrace, forever stay.

Through verdant banks, the wildflowers sway,
Coloring paths that lead astray.
Murmurs of rivers, soft and true,
Tell of the magic that lives in you.

## Fae Revels at Dusk

In twilight's glow, the fae take flight,
With laughter soft, they twirl in light.
A chorus hums, the night alive,
As dreams and magic intertwine and thrive.

With whispered spells, they weave the air,
Each shimmering dust, a secret shared.
They dance through shadows, free and bold,
In realms where stories once were told.

## Fables Woven in Twilight

In twilight's hush, old tales revive,
With woven threads of dreams we strive.
Each story spun in colors bright,
Against the canvas of the night.

The moonlit words, like gentle rain,
Bring forth the magic, ease the pain.
In every heart, a fable sown,
Awakens whispers, seeds are grown.

## The Dance of Fluttering Petals

Beneath the boughs, the petals glide,
A swirl of hues where dreams reside.
They spin and twirl in soft embrace,
As nature sings in fleeting grace.

A gentle breeze then calls their name,
Each bloom a dancer, wild and tame.
They scatter secrets on the breeze,
And grace the earth with scents that please.

## Secrets Beneath the Ancient Boughs

Beneath the roots, in shadowed glade,
Lies whispered lore that time has made.
Ancient boughs with stories deep,
Hold every secret that they keep.

In silence stirs the magic's hum,
Where cycles end and new ones come.
With every rustle, truths unfold,
In nature's grasp, life's tales retold.

# Whispers in the Enchanted Grove

In the grove where silence sighs,
Mossy carpets hide the ground,
Gentle breezes share old lies,
Magic lingers all around.

Dappled light breaks through the leaves,
Casting shadows, soft and light,
Nature weaves her silent weaves,
Cradling secrets, day and night.

Ancient trees stand tall and proud,
Guarding tales of years gone by,
Whispers stir beneath the shroud,
As the stars in twilight sigh.

Footsteps soft on nature's breath,
Echoes dance like fleeting dreams,
Life and death entwined in depth,
Flowing softly like the streams.

In the stillness, hearts will learn,
To embrace the gentle glow,
With each heart, a tale to turn,
In the grove, where whispers flow.

## Beneath the Green Canopy

Where sunlight filters, soft and sweet,
In the shade, the coolness holds,
Beneath the leaves, the heart will meet,
Nature's breath, a tale unfolds.

Vines entwine with whispered grace,
Chasing shadows, laughter spins,
Time stands still in this embrace,
As each rustling leaf begins.

Butterflies like dreams take flight,
Colors bright against the green,
In the hush of soft twilight,
Magic blooms where we have been.

Nature's canvas blooms in song,
With each note, the world ignites,
Beneath the canopy, we long,
For the peace of starry nights.

Amidst the vines, our spirits soar,
Holding hands beneath the sky,
In this grove, we ask for more,
For the love that will not die.

# Echoes of Stardust and Shadows

In the night where stardust glows,
Whispers of the moonlit tide,
Echoes dance where soft wind blows,
Spirits of the night abide.

Shadows play on ancient stones,
Flickering in the gentle breeze,
Carving pathways, silent tones,
Hidden truths beneath the trees.

Stars align in cosmic grace,
Guiding wanderers from afar,
In the darkness, find your place,
Many dreams will leave a scar.

Nature's hymn, a soothing balm,
Wraps us in its tender arms,
As the night brings peaceful calm,
With the forest's ancient charms.

In the echoes, stories wove,
Tales of love and timeless flows,
Underneath the starlit grove,
Life's mysterious beauty shows.

# The Gossamer Pathway

A pathway winds through silver mist,
Whispers weave in soft exchange,
Every turn, a secret kissed,
In this realm, the heart finds change.

Petals fall like tiny dreams,
Scattered through the verdant way,
Nature's art with quiet gleams,
Guiding hearts where shadows sway.

Gossamer threads of light entwine,
Leading souls to realms unknown,
In the dusk, our fates align,
With each step, we find our own.

Sunrise paints the skies anew,
Colors splashed with tender grace,
In this silver, morning dew,
We discover our true place.

Through the pathway, life will flow,
Each moment, a chance to soar,
In the gossamer glow, we know,
Every heartbeat opens doors.

## The Bursting Sky Beyond the Trees

The azure sweeps above, so wide,
Clouds dance in whispers, side by side.
Branches stretch towards the glowing light,
A promise of dreams in the coming night.

Birds take flight, with wings unfurled,
In the shade of green, a magic world.
Golden rays kiss the forest floor,
Nature's canvas, forevermore.

As dusk approaches, hues ignite,
A symphony plays, pure delight.
The sun dips low, painting the streams,
With colors rich, woven in dreams.

Whispers of breezes, soft and clear,
Calling the night, drawing us near.
The sky bursts forth with shades so rare,
Beyond the trees, magic fills the air.

## Flourishing Fables in Celestial Hues

In the twilight glow, tales unfold,
Celestial threads of stories told.
Stars sprinkle secrets upon the ground,
In whispers of light, hope is found.

Mythic creatures roam at night,
Painting dreams in silver light.
Their laughter echoes through the vale,
In flourishing fables, spirits sail.

With every brush of the cosmic hand,
(Imagination's boundless land).
Glimmers of wisdom, soft and bright,
Guide wandering hearts through the night.

Galaxies twirl in a dance divine,
Weaving timelines, yours and mine.
In cosmic tales, we lose our way,
Yet find our paths at the break of day.

# The Lilt of Laughter through Thickets

Through thickets dense, laughter weaves,
A melody sweet beneath the leaves.
Children's voices, ringing clear,
Echoing play, drawing us near.

Sunbeams prance on a dappled floor,
As joy spills over, we crave for more.
Whimsical winds hum along,
In heartbeats of nature, a lively song.

Tickling branches sway in glee,
Shadows stretch in playful spree.
With every giggle, the world grows bright,
A tapestry woven of pure delight.

In each corner, wonder prevails,
The lilt of laughter sails through trails.
Together we weave, stories as we roam,
Finding our joy in nature's home.

## Starlit Temptations in Sylvan Silence

In sylvan silence, stars emerge,
Flickering softly, urging a surge.
Night's embrace casts shadows long,
While whispers of dreams sing a song.

Beneath the boughs, temptations play,
In the coolness, shadows sway.
Secrets linger where the shadows dwell,
An alluring tale weaves a spell.

With every sigh of the ancient trees,
A breeze carries whispers, soft as pleas.
Dewdrops glisten like diamonds rare,
In starlit moments, magic fills the air.

Curiosity dances in the mind,
In every flicker, stories intertwined.
As the night deepens, we lose control,
Surrendering to the night's gentle pull.

# Driftwood Reveries Under the Larch

In shadows cast by larch and pine,
Driftwood whispers stories fine.
The river sings a gentle song,
Where echoes of lost dreams belong.

Beneath the boughs, the wildflowers sway,
Dancing softly, night to day.
Crickets chirp their evening tune,
Under the watch of a silver moon.

Ripples weave through sandy shores,
While twinkling stars align their scores.
Each fragment of wood holds time's trace,
A tapestry of nature's grace.

With every breath, the stillness grows,
In this sanctuary, silence flows.
I gather thoughts like drifting leaves,
In the embrace of ancient eaves.

Here in the cradle of larch's sway,
I find my heart, I find my way.
Driftwood dreams in twilight's glow,
Guide me where the wild winds blow.

## The Bloom of Celestial Wishes

In gardens where the starlight spills,
Celestial blooms defy the chills.
Petals whisper secrets bright,
Under the cloak of moonlit night.

Each blossom opens to the sky,
Where dreams of hope and wishes lie.
Soft fragrances in the breeze,
Carry tales of midnight pleas.

Colors dance in fragrant air,
As night unveils its tender care.
A symphony of fragrant bliss,
In shadows where the dreamers kiss.

Upon the dew-kissed petals lay,
The magic of the fading day.
With every bloom, a wish is cast,
In gardens tied to futures vast.

The celestial bloom, a soft delight,
Holds every heartbeat, every sight.
In every petal, stories weave,
Of all the dreams we dare believe.

# Twilight's Embrace in Fairy Glens

In glens where twilight shapes the earth,
The fairies dance, a spell of mirth.
Soft whispers float on gentle sighs,
As day bids farewell to the skies.

With every flicker of firefly light,
Magic awakens the coming night.
Beneath the leaves, a world concealed,
In twilight's arms, the fate revealed.

Mushrooms bloom in cerulean hues,
While dreams of starlit paths ensues.
Crisp air carries an ancient song,
In the fairy glen where we belong.

The brook sings soft a lullaby,
As shadows play where whispers lie.
Each crevice holds a tale untold,
Of love and courage, brave and bold.

In twilight's embrace, the heart finds peace,
As all its wanderings gently cease.
Fairy glens, a sacred space,
To bask forever in nature's grace.

## Starlit Pathways of Hidden Realms

Beneath a canopy of shimmering skies,
Starlit pathways beckon the wise.
With every step, a secret unfurls,
Guiding the wanderer through hidden worlds.

Whispers of wonders drift in the night,
As shadows weave magic, pure delight.
Footprints dusted in cosmic light,
Charting the course where dreams take flight.

The moon alights on pathways rare,
With silver threads that weave through air.
Each turn reveals a tale of lore,
Where hearts entwine forevermore.

In realms where time loses its thread,
With every heartbeat, new paths are bred.
Adventures await, a lingering call,
In starlit realms where shadows fall.

Embrace the journey, let it unfurl,
In starlit pathways, explore the swirl.
Each step you take, a story unfolds,
In hidden realms, where wonder beholds.

# Shadows of the Sylvan Realm

In the hush of twilight's glow,
Where ancient trees stand tall and proud,
Shadows dance in whispers low,
Embracing every earthy shroud.

Beneath the stars, the night unveils,
A tapestry of dreams foretold,
Mystic paths where silence trails,
Stories spun in hues of gold.

Crickets sing a serenade,
To the moon's soft, silver gaze,
While secrets in the glades cascade,
In nature's soft and tender ways.

River murmurs, tales untold,
Through the woods where spirits roam,
In the heart of forest bold,
Here, every soul finds their home.

So linger in this sylvan space,
Where shadows weave their silent art,
In the embrace of nature's grace,
The realm of dreams will not depart.

## Echoes of Ethereal Lullabies

In the night, a soft refrain,
Whispers drift like feathered light,
Cradled in a gentle pain,
Echoes born from endless night.

Moonlight bathes the silent grove,
Casting dreams on tender leaves,
Every star a story wove,
Where the heart of silence breathes.

Nightingale with velvet song,
Sings of love and lost delight,
In the woods where shadows long,
Meld with magic's purest light.

Ethereal sounds a lullaby,
Swaying gently through the glade,
Stirring souls as they reply,
To the serenade that's laid.

So close your eyes, let visions shine,
In the embrace of twilight's grace,
In echoes soft, our lives entwine,
Finding peace in every space.

## Threads of Starlight in the Canopy

Above the trees, the stars align,
Threads of silver, pure and bright,
Weaving dreams of fate divine,
In the velvet cloak of night.

Beneath the leaves, the earth does sigh,
As the moon spills gentle beams,
Starlight weaves a lullaby,
Guiding us through whispered dreams.

Through the branches, dances flow,
Elfin laughter in the breeze,
In this realm where spirits glow,
Time drifts softly, free and pleased.

Glimmering paths unveil their lore,
In this woodland, vast and deep,
Every step unlocks a door,
Where the heart learns how to leap.

So take my hand, let's wander far,
Through this tapestry we find,
In starlit strands, we are the star,
Connected, body, soul, and mind.

## Serenade of the Woodland Spirits

In the hush of forest's heart,
Woodland spirits sing their song,
In every shadow, they impart,
Melodies that linger long.

Dancing leaves in twilight's glow,
Sway with whispers from above,
Every breeze a gentle flow,
Carrying the scent of love.

Through the thickets, laughter plays,
As the nightingale takes flight,
Rustling branches weave in praise,
To the magic of the night.

Frogs and crickets join the choir,
Nature's symphony unfolds,
Softly kindling hearts' desire,
In the stories that it holds.

So listen close, let spirit guide,
In the dance of night divine,
With each note, let souls confide,
In this serenade, we shine.

## The Embrace of Glittering Meadows

In fields where sunlight dances bright,
Golden blooms catch morning light,
Whispers of the gentle breeze,
Send sweet secrets through the trees.

A carpet of colors, wide and free,
Nature's canvas, wild and spree,
Where laughter spills from skies so blue,
And every heart finds joy anew.

Butterflies flit on wings of grace,
In this enchanting, vibrant space,
Dreams unfold in hues of gold,
Stories of love and life retold.

With every step, the earth does sing,
To the rhythm of the joyful spring,
Heartbeats echo in harmony,
In meadows vast, we're truly free.

So linger here, let worries cease,
In nature's arms, discover peace,
As the glittering meadows sway,
Embrace the beauty of today.

## Enchantment in Stillness

In the hush of evening's glow,
Where the twilight shadows flow,
Time suspends in soft embrace,
Finding solace in this space.

Moonlight kisses silent streams,
Starlight weaves enchanting dreams,
Each moment holds a sacred pause,
Nature offers silent applause.

Whispers travel on the air,
Stories hidden everywhere,
In the stillness, heartbeats blend,
As night descends, the world transcends.

Crickets sing their softest tune,
Underneath the silver moon,
In this quiet, magic glows,
Enchantment wraps around our souls.

When dawn breaks, it softly steers,
We carry shadows, calm our fears,
For in stillness, truth resides,
An endless journey, where love guides.

# Lore of the Woodland Nymphs

In woodland depths, where shadows play,
Nymphs weave stories, night and day,
With laughter bright as morning dew,
They guard the secrets old and new.

Among the trees, their presence glows,
In whispers soft, the magic flows,
A gentle touch, a playful tease,
In ancient groves, their spirits freeze.

They weave the tales of long ago,
In every leaf, their voices flow,
From roots to sky, they sing their song,
In harmony where all belong.

By moonlit streams, they dance and twirl,
In a timeless, wondrous whirl,
With every breeze, a magic spark,
Illuminates the forest dark.

Beneath the stars, the legends grow,
In every pulse, their whispers show,
The lore of nymphs, both wild and free,
In nature's heart, our spirits see.

# Mysteries of the Shimmering Glade

In the glade where secrets hide,
Where sunlight filters, soft and wide,
Mossy carpets cradle the earth,
In shimmering light, a silent birth.

Wanderers pause to catch their breath,
Enchanted by the air of myth,
Every ripple, a tales' embrace,
In hidden paths, we find our place.

The ferns unfold, like stories told,
Through whispers of the brave and bold,
Crystalline waters hold their gaze,
Reflecting dreams in whispered phase.

Ghostly figures drift and sway,
In twilight's cloak, they softly play,
Unraveling threads of time and space,
In this glade, we find our grace.

So linger here, let nature speak,
In every sigh, the answers seek,
For within the glade, the heart does know,
The mysteries of life's gentle flow.

# Secrets of the Sylvan Realm

Whispers dance among the trees,
Ancient tales carried on the breeze.
Shadows hide in emerald hues,
Nature's secrets, only few choose.

Starlit paths that softly glow,
Guarded by the winds that blow.
Hidden magic, softly spun,
In the stillness, dreams begun.

Among the roots, the stories creep,
Echoes of the night, they seep.
Elusive sprites and wandering light,
Guide the way through dark and night.

With every step, the forest sighs,
Beneath the gaze of silver skies.
A melody of nature's charm,
Embracing all within its arm.

In this realm of whispered dreams,
Truth resides in flowing streams.
Follow where the heart does lead,
In the sylvan, find your creed.

## Lullabies from the Faerie Glade

Crickets sing a gentle tune,
Underneath the watching moon.
Softly sway the dancing leaves,
In this space, the heart believes.

Twinkling lights like stars descend,
In the night, where dreams blend.
Faerie laughter fills the air,
Bringing peace beyond compare.

Lullabies of night unfold,
Stories sweet, forever told.
Wrapped in dreams, the world slows down,
As slumber weaves a velvet crown.

Here in this enchanted place,
Time stands still, a soft embrace.
Whispers of the earth and sky,
Cradle wishes as they fly.

In the glade, all worries cease,
Finding solace, finding peace.
With each note, the heart takes wing,
In the night, the faeries sing.

# Tapestry of Moonlit Wishes

Silver threads in shadows weave,
A tapestry of dreams conceived.
Moonlit whispers fill the air,
Each heart's wish, a precious prayer.

Stars aligned with soft intent,
Guiding thoughts where time is spent.
Night enfolds the weary soul,
In its arms, we're made whole.

Fragments of the night unfurl,
Secrets hidden in the swirl.
Voices call from realms afar,
Unlocking doors with every star.

With every gleam, our hopes take flight,
Soaring high into the night.
Crafted dreams like jewels bright,
In the hush, they dance with light.

Underneath the watchful sky,
Wishes, like soft breezes, cry.
In the moon's embrace, we trust,
Tapestry of love and lust.

## Flutters of the Ethereal Wings

Gossamer threads, a fleeting sight,
Ethereal beings take to flight.
In the dusky evening's glow,
Whispers carried where dreams go.

Wings that shimmer, soft as air,
Dancing gently, without a care.
Nature's song calls them to weave,
In the tales that night conceives.

With a flutter, they glide near,
Serenade the world we hold dear.
Echoes of a hidden grace,
Kiss the beauty of this place.

Through the twilight's gentle hush,
Hope awakens with a rush.
Magic flows within their play,
Filling hearts with brave array.

As the stars begin to wane,
Wings retreat, like soft-spun rain.
In their wake, a longing stays,
For the light of magic days.

## The Ethereal Light Between the Trees

In the forest where whispers roam,
Sunlight dances, nature's home.
Leaves are painted with golden hues,
As shadows waltz with morning dews.

Branches weep with tales untold,
Emerald canopies, secrets unfold.
Breeze carries laughter, soft and sweet,
A melody where earth and sky meet.

Glimmers peek through the rustling green,
Mysteries linger, serene and keen.
Footsteps trace where fairies play,
In this twilight, night steals the day.

Ghostly whispers in twilight's glow,
Lost in reverie as the soft winds blow.
Ethereal light guides the way,
Through the trees, dreams gently swayed.

As night falls, the stars awake,
Nature breathes, the silence breaks.
In the heart of woods, peace is found,
With every rustle, love surrounds.

## The Enigma of Twinkling Trails

Upon the path where footfalls fade,
Stars above in glimmering cascade.
Each twinkle whispers a secret song,
As shadows shift, we wander along.

Moonlight weaves through the dusky air,
Guiding souls with tender care.
Silver beams on the winding way,
Illuminate night, dispel the gray.

Crickets chirp in harmony's dance,
Echoing dreams that weave and prance.
Every gleam tells a tale anew,
Hiding wonders for hearts so true.

Footprints lost in the velvet night,
Leading onward, out of sight.
Whispers call from the depths of time,
Inviting souls to grasp the rhyme.

Set adrift in a cosmic sea,
These trails unveil infinity.
With every star, the mystery grows,
In the dance of light, the last one goes.

## Meadow's Heartbeat Under Silver Skies

In the meadow where wildflowers play,
Sunshine spills in a bright ballet.
Breezes murmur through fragrant blooms,
Nature's pulse in the quiet rooms.

Clouds drift lazily, soft as dreams,
Casting shadows, painting streams.
Grass whispers stories, age-old and wise,
Under the watch of awakening skies.

A lone bird sings a morning song,
With every note, the world feels strong.
Colors blend in a gentle sway,
In harmony, they dance and play.

Butterflies flutter, a painted flight,
Kissing petals, a dazzling sight.
Meadow holds the heartbeat's grace,
In each moment, a timeless space.

As twilight comes, the hues grow deep,
Nature's lullaby begins to seep.
In the meadow's embrace, we find,
A tranquil peace for the wandering mind.

# Whirling Colors of Dreaming Glades

In glades where dreams take wing and soar,
Colors swirl, a vibrant lore.
Whispers of twilight paint the scene,
A magic realm where souls convene.

Dancing shadows flicker and blend,
With every turn, the colors bend.
Lavender skies meet the emerald floor,
In a symphony, a silent roar.

Wildflowers bloom in a wild spree,
Caressing breezes, wild and free.
Each petal tells a story bold,
Of adventures that the heart can hold.

Glistening dewdrops catch the light,
Sparkling gems in the coming night.
Whirling colors, a wondrous sight,
In dreaming glades, life feels so right.

As darkness falls, the stars ignite,
Painting dreams in the canvas of night.
In every hue, in every sway,
The essence of life, here to stay.

# The Gossamer Wings of Hope

Upon the dawn where dreams take flight,
Soft whispers dance in morning light.
Wings of gossamer, light as air,
Lifting our hearts beyond despair.

In quiet moments, visions gleam,
Threads of silver weave the dream.
Hope flickers bright, a distant star,
Guiding us from where we are.

In shadows cast by doubt and fear,
The glimmers of faith draw us near.
To reach the skies, we spread our wings,
In every soul, a songbird sings.

With every challenge that we face,
We find our strength, we find our grace.
For in the depths, a spark ignites,
The gossamer wings to endless heights.

So let us soar beyond the maze,
Embrace the hope that brightly stays.
With every breath, we'll rise and shine,
In gossamer dreams, our paths align.

## Secrets Carried by the Zephyr

Beneath the clouds, the zephyr sighs,
Whispers of secrets drift and rise.
Carrying tales of days gone by,
In gentle breezes, soft and spry.

Through emerald leaves, it softly weaves,
Stirring the heart, rustling trees.
Secrets of lovers, promises sweet,
Carried afar on nimble feet.

It dances lightly on jasmine air,
A fragrant secret, light as prayer.
In every corner, it finds its way,
Through laughter's echo, where children play.

The zephyr knows what hearts might yearn,
In every flutter, a lesson learned.
With every gust, a memory stirs,
A symphony of life occurs.

So listen close as the winds do tell,
Of dreams fulfilled and hope as well.
In every whisper, a chance to see,
The secrets carried on the zephyr's glee.

## In the Heart of Faery Whispers

In twilight shades, where shadows bend,
The faery whispers start to blend.
A symphony of soft delight,
In the heart of the coming night.

Among the ferns, where secrets lie,
Beneath the stars, the stories fly.
Gossamer threads weave a tale,
Of ancient magic, pure and pale.

With every sigh, the night unfolds,
A tapestry of dreams retold.
Faery laughter fills the glade,
In every shadow, magic laid.

Their voices soft, like breezes fleet,
In the heart of woods, they gently greet.
The quietude holds mysteries deep,
In the faery realm, where wonders sleep.

So delve within, let go the fear,
For in their song, the world is clear.
In the heart of faery whispers' light,
We find our truth, our endless flight.

## Reveries Beneath the Elder Tree

Beneath the boughs of ancient grace,
Reveries waltz in a sacred space.
The elder tree, with wisdom old,
Holds secrets of the earth, untold.

In dappled light, the moments weave,
Dreams woven through what we believe.
Leaves murmur tales of days gone past,
In every rustle, echoes cast.

Laughter of children, faint yet clear,
Lingers in the branches near.
The roots hold stories, deep and wide,
Of love and loss, of hearts that bide.

A quiet place where spirits roam,
In nature's arms, we find our home.
With every breath, the tales revive,
Beneath the elder, we feel alive.

So come and rest where shadows play,
Let the mind wander, drift away.
Reveries beneath the ancient tree,
A sanctuary for you and me.

# A Journey through Whispering Winds

In twilight's glow, the paths unwind,
Where every rustle speaks so kind.
The air is thick with tales untold,
As shadows dance, both brave and bold.

We follow trails where echoes play,
And listen close to what they say.
A breeze that bends the branches low,
Guides us through this mystic flow.

With every step, the whispers tease,
They wrap around like summer's breeze.
A journey carved in nature's grace,
In memory's arms, we find our place.

Through leafy paths where secrets hide,
The heart and soul of earth collide.
Each rustling leaf a story spun,
As twilight fades, our quest begun.

So onward still, the stars ignite,
The winds will howl, the dawn will bite.
A journey made with every breath,
In whispering winds, we find our depth.

## Soft Footfalls of Enigmatic Beings

In the hush where shadows dwell,
Footfalls echo like a spell.
Through the mist, they weave and glide,
Enigmatic whispers by our side.

A shimmer brushed by moonlit beams,
Carrying secrets, hopes, and dreams.
They tread upon the leaf-carpeted floor,
Each step a tale, a hidden lore.

Among the ferns, the magic hides,
Guided by the spirit that abides.
Soft footfalls, like a lover's sigh,
In the glow of stars, they drift and fly.

In twilight's embrace, they sway and sigh,
Lurking gently where shadows lie.
A journey shared with the unseen kin,
In quiet woods, the dance begins.

Together in the night's soft grace,
We wander through this enchanted space.
With every breath, the world feels new,
Soft footfalls lead us, ever true.

## The Pull of the Enchanted Breeze

An ethereal sigh, a gentle pull,
The enchanted breeze, so soft and full.
It carries dreams from near and far,
Guiding souls like a shimmering star.

With whispers low, it calls to me,
A serenade from the ancient tree.
It stirs the leaves, the petals dance,
In a world awash with twilight's trance.

Each breath unveils a hidden path,
A journey born from nature's wrath.
The winds entwine, weaving through,
Drawing us close to realms anew.

Beneath the sky, where hopes take flight,
The enchanted breeze, our guiding light.
It sings of stories yet to bloom,
Filling the air with sweet perfume.

To follow where the spirits roam,
To let the breeze lead us back home.
A dance with fate amidst the trees,
Forever caught in the enchanted breeze.

## Pollen-Laden Secrets of the Forest

Amidst the boughs, the air is sweet,
With pollen dancing at our feet.
A tapestry of fragrant dreams,
Beneath the sun, everything gleams.

The forest whispers, secrets shared,
In every bloom, a promise bared.
With wings that flutter soft and low,
Nature's symphony begins to flow.

Each petal holds a tale of old,
Of lives entwined in beauty bold.
Upon the breeze, the stories drift,
In shimmering light, the spirits lift.

Pollen-laden, the air's alive,
In this wild haven, we will thrive.
Through labyrinth paths, let curiosity spark,
In every crevice, a secret arc.

So let us wander, hand in hand,
Through secret glades in this enchanted land.
For in the forest, where dreams do blend,
Pollen-laden secrets never end.

### Glistening Shadows of the Night

In the quiet glow of twilight,
Shadows dance upon the ground,
Whispers linger in the stillness,
As stars begin to twirl around.

Moonbeams weave a silver tapestry,
Drawing lines through darkened trees,
Gentle breezes carry secrets,
Filling hearts with silent pleas.

Each shadow holds a story,
Of days and nights long past,
Echoes whisper through the ages,
In a world forever vast.

Cloaked in mystery and wonder,
Night generously unfolds,
A canvas rich with lifetimes,
In hues of deep and bold.

So let us wander through the starlight,
Embrace the night so bright,
For in glistening shadows dwelling,
Our souls take flight in flight.

## Kaleidoscope of Enchanted Whispers

Colors swirl in vibrant patterns,
Dreams take wing upon the breeze,
Stories flit through leaf and flower,
In a realm where magic frees.

Voices weave a gentle chorus,
Threads of laughter, sighs, and tears,
A tapestry of nature's heart,
Binding hopes with whispered fears.

Each petal tells a secret tale,
Of sunlit days and rainy nights,
Captured in a moment's bliss,
In the dance of pure delights.

Amidst the rustling leaves we wander,
In a world that softly glows,
Kaleidoscopic visions shimmer,
Where every heartbeat knows.

So pause and listen to the whispers,
Let your spirit intertwine,
With the enchanted hues of nature,
In this magic, brightly shine.

# Secrets Sown with Moonlit Seeds

Underneath the silvered sky,
Secrets whispered on the breeze,
Moonlight bathes the sleeping earth,
In a glow that never flees.

Winds carry tales from long ago,
Sown in gardens of the night,
Every shadow a reminder,
Of patterns etched in purest light.

In the hush of quiet hours,
Dreams take root beneath our feet,
Nurtured by the starlit glow,
In a sanctuary so sweet.

The night unveils her hidden truths,
As flowers bloom in gentle sighs,
Each petal holds a secret wish,
Beneath the tapestry of skies.

So gather these moonlit whispers,
Plant them gently in your heart,
For the seeds of night will flourish,
In the dreams that love impart.

## Tales Spun in Nature's Embrace

In the forest, where shadows blend,
Nature whispers tales untold,
Each leaf a page, each breeze a word,
Mysteries in green and gold.

Sunlight dances through the branches,
Weaving stories, bright and clear,
In every rustle, every ripple,
Life unravels, drawing near.

Rivers hum their ancient verses,
Mountains stand in solemn grace,
All unite in nature's chorus,
Time suspended in this place.

Here the heart finds sweet connection,
With every ripple, leaf, and stone,
In nature's embrace, we gather strength,
In quiet moments, we are known.

So let us wander, hand in hand,
In the tales that only trees can tell,
For in these woods, a world awaits,
Where every soul can find its spell.

# Spirals of Magic in Sultry Air

Beneath the twilight's woven glow,
Whispers swirl in the heated breeze.
Enchanted trails where shadows flow,
Dance with secrets among the leaves.

Crickets sing a soft tune's caress,
Fireflies twinkle, casting delight.
In the heart of the night, we confess,
Magic spins in the calm of light.

The air thickens with sweet perfume,
Laughter echoes through the dark.
In wild dreams, we dare to zoom,
And lose ourselves, leaving a mark.

Waves of warmth in a gentle haze,
Murmurs play upon the ground.
Eyes closed, we lose our maze,
In spirals of magic, we are found.

## Moonshadow Against the Ancient Bark

Silent watch beneath the moon,
Branches twist in whispered sighs.
Time stands still, a gentle rune,
As secrets dance beneath the skies.

Bark like wisdom, strong and deep,
Eons old with stories sown.
In moonshadow, dreams take leap,
In night's embrace, we feel at home.

The nightingale sings soft and low,
A melody of shadows and light.
In this cocoon, the spirits flow,
Guiding hearts through the still night.

Ancient trees, keepers of lore,
Their arms cradle the stars' fall.
In moonlit glow, we seek for more,
Love and magic fuse, enthrall.

## Enthralled by the Faerie Tides

A shimmer dances on the brook,
Where faeries ride the gentle waves.
In hidden nooks, we dare to look,
And find the joy that nature saves.

Moonlit waters pulse and shine,
Each ripple sings a lullaby.
With laughter soft, the faeries twine,
Their ebbing song floats through the sky.

We chase the starlight, wild and free,
Each moment pulls us further in.
The ocean hums, a symphony,
Where every wave stirs loss and win.

Women of the tides, we sway,
Drawing breath from thalassic dreams.
In the twilight, we wish to stay,
Enthralled by all the faerie schemes.

## Honeyed Sighs of the Grove

In the grove where blossoms twine,
Honey drips from petals bright.
Softly hums a steady line,
Nature's song in warm twilight.

The scent of nectar fills the air,
Bees dance lightly, weaving tales.
In golden hues, we breathe and share,
Where laughter drifts like sweetened gales.

Rustling leaves in a serene chart,
Whispers of the age-old tree.
From every branch, a sacred part,
Tells the world of you and me.

In honeyed sighs, our spirits blend,
Caught in laughter, pure and free.
With each embrace, our roots extend,
In this grove, our hearts agree.

# Murmurs in the Woodland Vigil

In twilight's hush, the whispers play,
Leaves rustle softly, night meets day.
Creatures stir in shadowed glades,
Nature's song, as dusk invades.

A brook does babble, secrets kept,
Beneath the boughs where fairies slept.
The stars peek down, a twinkling light,
A guardian's watch on this sacred night.

Every breath brings tales untold,
In emerald realms of dreams unfold.
Murmurs dance on cool night air,
As magic swirls, here, everywhere.

In the hush, a flicker glows,
The heartbeat of the forest flows.
Whispers of the ancient trees,
Carried gently on the breeze.

When dawn arrives, the silence breaks,
With rosy hues, the daylight wakes.
Yet echoes linger, soft and sweet,
In woodland vigil, hearts still meet.

## The Lure of the Hidden Grove

Beyond the thicket, secrets lie,
In hidden groves where fairies fly.
The air is thick with ancient lore,
Inviting souls to seek for more.

Mossy paths and tangled vines,
Whispers beckon from the pines.
Each step draws closer to the heart,
Where shadows dance and dreams take part.

Sunbeams filter through the leaves,
Dancing light that gently weaves.
Echoes call from deep within,
Enticing journeys to begin.

Within the grove, time seems to stall,
As nature's whispers softly call.
In every heart, a longing glows,
For hidden truths the spirit knows.

To chase the light through shades of green,
To find the magic, pure and keen.
The lure of places unexplored,
In the hidden grove, our dreams restored.

# Faery Lights on a Starlit Path

Along the path where stars descend,
Small lights flicker, bright as friends.
Guiding footsteps through the night,
With whispers soft, a sweet delight.

Each faery glow a beckoning spark,
Illuminating dreams in the dark.
A trail of wonders, a celestial dance,
Inviting hearts to take a chance.

Moonlit dances and laughter shared,
In emerald realms where few have dared.
The starlit path, a cosmic weave,
In every twist, a chance to believe.

Fluttering wings, a gentle breeze,
Carrying messages through the trees.
Every shadow, every sigh,
A promise whispered under the sky.

As dawn approaches, lights will fade,
Yet memories linger, not betrayed.
The magic lives in each soft glow,
On the starlit path where dreamers go.

## The Garden Where Wishes Bloom

In gentle soil, where dreams take seed,
A garden thrives of every need.
Petals whisper, secrets sweet,
Promises made where heartbeats meet.

Colors burst in joyful array,
A tapestry bright, come what may.
Every bloom, a wish set free,
Growing wild in harmony.

Amidst the vines, hope intertwines,
Echoing laughter in soft designs.
In the stillness, magic stirs,
As the heart listens to what occurs.

Sunshine drapes the sacred ground,
In this haven, solace found.
With each petal fluttering down,
The garden wears a tranquil crown.

As twilight falls, the stars emerge,
In the garden where wishes surge.
A space to dream, to bloom anew,
A sanctuary for hearts so true.

# The Hidden Grove of Dreamweavers

In the grove where shadows play,
Dreams weave softly night and day.
Whispers blend with twilight's song,
In this realm where hearts belong.

Trees adorned with silver light,
Guarding secrets, pure and bright.
Steps echoing on mossy ground,
In this haven, peace is found.

Stars above, like gems they gleam,
Carving paths of a hidden dream.
Hearts align in sacred space,
Together in this tranquil place.

Calm embrace of nature's art,
Here, the world can restart.
Magic lingers in each sigh,
As the moon drifts softly by.

## Celestial Chimes of Forgotten Tales

Beneath the stars, chimes softly ring,
Echoes of tales that time would bring.
Whispers dance on the breeze so light,
In the hush of a velvet night.

Lost stories from ages past,
In the darkness, they are cast.
Each note a spark, a flame of old,
In the silence, secrets unfold.

Moonlit paths of shimmering dreams,
Woven through with silver beams.
Hearts remember, though they stray,
The songs of night will guide the way.

Listen close to the fading sound,
Where forgotten hopes are tightly bound.
Through the echoes, journeys start,
Binding souls, uniting hearts.

## Traces of Magic in Morning Dew

Morning breaks with gentle grace,
In each droplet, dreams embrace.
Whispers of the night give way,
To the light of another day.

Dewdrops glisten on vibrant leaves,
Carrying whispers of forgotten eves.
A sparkle here, a shimmer there,
In this realm of magic rare.

Footprints fade but stories remain,
As the sun breaks through the rain.
Nature's palette begins to bloom,
Chasing away all hints of gloom.

Hope is born with each new ray,
Waking dreams that softly lay.
In the dance of light and hue,
Traces of magic start anew.

## Pathways Through the Whispering Woods

In the woods where secrets dwell,
Nature speaks, a silent spell.
Paths meander, winding low,
Guiding hearts where few may go.

Leaves murmur tales of joy and woe,
In the depths where shadows grow.
Branches sway in gentle breeze,
Echoing the whispers of trees.

Footfalls soft on earth's embrace,
Each step leads to a hidden place.
Woven dreams in twilight's glow,
As the wilds around us flow.

A journey wrapped in nature's grace,
Discovering time's secret face.
Through the woods, our spirits soar,
In the heart of the forest's lore.

## Twilight Facets of Enchanted Hope

In the glow of the fading light,
Dreams weave through the silent night.
Stars awaken, shyly gleam,
Illuminating every dream.

Whispers dance on the gentle breeze,
Carrying secrets among the trees.
Hope shimmers in the twilight's embrace,
A soft smile on the moon's face.

Moments linger, like a sweet sigh,
As shadows stretch and gently lie.
Each heartbeat a silent prayer,
To the wishes floating in the air.

The world hushes, wrapped in peace,
As the evening's magic finds release.
Colors blend in a painter's hand,
Creating beauty across the land.

In these facets of twilight's hue,
Hope awakens, fresh and anew.
We find solace, as time flows slow,
In enchanted realms where wonders grow.

## Where Innocence and Magic Combine

In a garden where laughter plays,
Children's joy fills endless days.
Magic lingers on the breeze,
A world of wonder, hearts at ease.

Beneath the boughs of ancient trees,
Dreams are spun like playful bees.
Imagination soars, takes flight,
Painting visions in pure delight.

Petals shimmer with morning dew,
Whispers of magic come into view.
Innocence glows in every glance,
A secret wink, a sweet romance.

Fireflies twinkle, an evening show,
Guiding our hearts where dreams can flow.
Hand in hand, we wander free,
In a realm where all can see.

Where innocence dances with the night,
And magic glows in soft twilight.
We are lost in the wonder sublime,
In this sacred realm of time.

## Luminescent Trails of Lost Lullabies

Echoes of whispers drift through the air,
Lullabies linger, woven with care.
Stars are harbingers of tales untold,
In the night, memories unfold.

Footprints shimmer on a silver path,
Tracing the music of gentle wrath.
Each note a sigh, each chord a tear,
Speaking the language of love and fear.

In shadows cast by the moon's bright glow,
Lost lullabies begin to flow.
Their melodies weave through the night,
Resonating with fragile light.

Time fades softly, like a sweet tune,
Cradled gently under the moon.
In this space where dreams reside,
A tapestry of hope will abide.

The trails we leave, luminous yet fleeting,
Carry the magic of love's sweet beating.
In every whisper, a harmony lies,
A promise held in the brightest skies.

## Flickers of Light in Soft Dusk


As the day kisses the night goodbye,
Flickers of light begin to sigh.
Stars awaken with twinkling grace,
Filling the dark with their embrace.

Golden hues turn into deep blue,
Where whispers of twilight beckon you.
Clouds drift softly, stitched with gold,
Stories of dreams waiting to unfold.

Each flicker holds a gentle spark,
Guiding wanderers through the dark.
In silence, magic dances bright,
Chasing shadows with pure delight.

Threads of dusk weave a tender spell,
Filling the air with tales to tell.
In the quiet, hearts align,
Finding solace in love's design.

As night settles, we find our peace,
In flickers of light, all worries cease.
Together we share this moment true,
Under the canvas of twilight's hue.

## The Eldergrove's Soft Breath

In the hush of twilight's grace,
Whispers dance from tree to tree.
Ancient roots in tranquil space,
Breathe the secrets of the lea.

Mossy blankets, emerald hue,
Cradle dreams of nights long gone.
In the mist, the shadows brew,
While the stars respond with song.

Moonlight kisses undergrowth,
Delicate as a sigh.
Each bark holds a tale, a oath,
Of the earth, both low and high.

Gentle breezes weave the air,
Carrying scents of decay.
Nature's heart can't help but share,
The wisdom gleaned from day.

Time meanders in this space,
Where the old embrace the new.
Feel the magic, find your place,
In the Eldergrove's soft view.

## Light Through Lattice of Leaves

Golden beams break through the boughs,
Creating patterns on the ground.
Nature's canvas softly allows,
A symphony of light, profound.

Each leaf has a tale to tell,
Of sunshine captured in their veins.
In this haven, all is well,
As time with openness remains.

Flickers dance in dappled hues,
Glimmers bright as daylight fades.
In the silence, nature brews,
A soft melody that cascades.

Branches sway with whispered cheer,
Brought forth by the gentle breeze.
In this realm, the world feels near,
As joy invites us to seize.

Light through lattice, pure delight,
Guides the wandering soul within.
Embrace the magic of the light,
Let serendipity begin.

# Faeries Upon a Gentle Whirl

In moonlit glades where shadows play,
Faeries dance and twirl about.
With laughter bright, they light the way,
Painting dreams with silver sprout.

Delicate wings in twilight glow,
Flutter softly through the air.
Each gentle dip, each fleeting flow,
Whispers secrets, soft and rare.

Evening blooms release their scent,
Inviting sprites to join the night.
Nature's breath is sweetly pent,
As magic rises to new height.

In the heart of the starlit woods,
Watch the faeries form their ring.
Amidst the trees and soothing broods,
Joyful echoes start to sing.

Life's true enchantment in their haste,
Is a spark that won't confine.
In this flurry, time is laced,
With wonder, ineffable, divine.

# The Secret Song of Wildflowers


In the meadow, petals sway,
Colors burst like morning light.
Whispers of the earth at play,
Crafting beauty, pure delight.

Every bloom sings a soft tune,
Gentle notes on zephyrs ride.
Beneath the warm embrace of noon,
Colors blend with nature's pride.

Bees hum along, a buzzing choir,
While butterflies dance in the breeze.
Wildflowers lift their heads, aspire,
To tell stories with such ease.

Through the grasses, secrets spread,
In their hues, the heart will find.
A melody that softly bled,
With every petal intertwined.

So stop and listen, take a pause,
To the song that nature sings.
In the wild, there are no laws,
Just the joy that living brings.

# Whispers of Enchanted Meadows

In meadows green where wildflowers sway,
Soft breezes carry whispers of play.
Sunlight dances on petals bright,
Nature's chorus sings of delight.

Beneath the oak, shadows weave,
Stories untold, weaves hearts believe.
In every rustle, a secret told,
In the warm embrace of the gold.

Streams that giggle as they flow,
Lily pads float in a gentle show.
Butterflies twirl in the golden rays,
Filling the world with their airy ballet.

As twilight descends with a sigh,
Stars awaken in the velvet sky.
Crickets chirp their nightly song,
A lullaby where dreams belong.

In enchanted meadows, forever we'll roam,
Innature's arms, we find our home.
With each whisper, our spirits soar,
In the embrace of the evermore.

# Secrets in the Moonlit Glade

In the glade where shadows dance,
Silver beams cast a fleeting glance.
Whispers linger on the breeze,
Carrying tales of ancient trees.

Night blooms open, petals wide,
Under the stars, where secrets hide.
Flickering lights, a firefly's flight,
Guiding the heart through the velvet night.

A hidden path leads us away,
Where echoing silence begins to play.
Footsteps soft on mossy ground,
In this sanctuary, peace is found.

Mystic creatures flicker in sight,
Guardians of the magic bright.
Each breath taken, a story unfolds,
In the moonlit glade, where wonder beholds.

As dawn's first glow begins to creep,
The secrets of night safely keep.
In the heart of the glade, dreams reside,
Where the moon and the earth confide.

# Dances of Delicate Fantasies

In a world brushed soft with morning mist,
Dreams unfurl in the sun's warm kiss.
Twirls of petals, in the air they twine,
A ballet of shadows, perfectly divine.

Each flutter whispers tales anew,
Of delicate fantasies that come into view.
Glimmers and sparkles scatter the ground,
In this realm of magic, joy is found.

Laughter echoes through the whirls,
As leaves above begin to swirl.
Echoes of sunlight, in glistening streams,
Awakening hearts to whimsical dreams.

The breeze carries secrets of joy,
Dancing along like a playful toy.
With every moment, our spirits rise,
In the dance of the day, beneath the skies.

As twilight beckons with a gentle peace,
The world softens, and all fears cease.
In dances of dreams, we find our place,
In the delicate embrace of nature's grace.

# The Laughter of Blossom Spirits

In gardens where the blossoms bloom,
Laughter springs, dispelling gloom.
Petals twinkle in soft sunlight,
Each burst of color, a pure delight.

With every breeze, echoes of glee,
Tiny spirits flit, wild and free.
Over the flowers, they twirl and spin,
In a joyous dance, where dreams begin.

Sways of daisies, nodding in time,
With whispers of laughter, a sweet chime.
The fragrance of petals, soft and dear,
Fills the heart with summer cheer.

In twilight's glow, as day says goodbye,
The spirits gather under the sky.
Their laughter lingers, soft like a sigh,
Echoing gently where memories lie.

Through seasons changing, their joy remains,
In the songs of the breeze, in the gentle rains.
The laughter of blossoms in every heart,
A reminder of love, never to part.

## A Spellbound Meeting of Myth and Moon

Underneath the silver glow,
Twilight whispers secrets low,
Creatures dance in shadows deep,
While ancient echoes softly weep.

A spell is cast with every gaze,
In the night's enchanting haze,
Myths entwined with lunar light,
Creating dreams that take to flight.

Stars align in cosmic rhyme,
Tales of yore, lost in time,
Fables told by the moon's embrace,
In this enchanted, sacred space.

Between the worlds, a door swings wide,
Where spirits of the night abide,
They beckon softly, hearts take flight,
In this realm of pure delight.

Hand in hand, we seek the lore,
Of forest paths and ocean's floor,
Together we shall weave our tale,
As gentle winds begin to sail.

## The Realm Beyond the Misty Edge

In shadowed glens where whispers roam,
A hidden world has found its home,
Where dreams are born and shadows play,
In the mist that hides the day.

Softly creeping, the fog descends,
A dance of light that never ends,
Through tangled woods and secret streams,
A place alive with ancient dreams.

Forgotten paths of twilight's grace,
Lead to the heart of this sacred space,
All who wander, lost in thought,
Discover treasures time forgot.

Voices call from beyond the veil,
Echoes of a timeless tale,
Guide the way with gentle care,
To realms of magic everywhere.

With every step, the wonders grow,
As secrets wait, a soft hello,
A journey's end and a new start,
In the realm beyond the heart.

## Lightly Treading on Faerie Ground


On dew-kissed grass, we pause to tread,
With whispers of the fae ahead,
Where sunlight beams on emerald glade,
And ancient spells are softly laid.

Glimmers spark in playful light,
As shadows twirl in pure delight,
Each bubble bursts with laughter fine,
A moment caught in velvet twine.

Through twisted roots and winding lanes,
A world of magic still remains,
Beneath the boughs of elder trees,
Where time is held by gentle breeze.

With hands outstretched, we touch the air,
And feel the pulse of magic there,
A faerie song upon the breeze,
Whispers echo through the trees.

We linger long in this embrace,
In faerie land, a sacred space,
With hearts like flowers, brightly found,
In harmony on faerie ground.

# The Horizon of Forgotten Magic

Across the dawn, where legends dwell,
Lies a horizon, whispers tell,
Of magic lost, yet found anew,
In every heart, a spark of blue.

Waves crash softly on the shore,
Echoes of the tales of yore,
As colors blend in vibrant hues,
A canvas rich with mystic clues.

The breeze carries a gentle tune,
A lullaby beneath the moon,
Inviting wanderers to explore,
The beauty of forgotten lore.

In the distance, shadows dance,
Awakening a fleeting chance,
To glimpse the wonders lost in time,
On the edge of dreams that brightly climb.

So take a step into the light,
Where magic stirs beyond the night,
And find your place within the weave,
On horizons where all believe.

# Songs of the Twilight Fey

Whispers dance on evening breeze,
Where shadows weave through ancient trees.
The fey sing soft in twilight's glow,
As secrets stir in twilight's flow.

Moonbeams brush the gentle ground,
In the hush where magic's found.
Glimmers flicker in twilight's hand,
Calling forth the dreamer's land.

With laughter laced in starlit air,
The fae invite with whispered flair.
Let your heart break free from night,
And wander where spirits take flight.

In this realm where time stands still,
Hope and wonder gently thrill.
Join the dance of night's embrace,
And find your place in twilight's space.

## The Glimmers of Daybreak Mystique

The dawn unfolds with softest grace,
As sunbeams stretch to warm the place.
Petals open, fresh and bright,
Kissing dewdrops in morning light.

Whispers of the night now fade,
In colors vivid, dreams delayed.
The world awakens with a sigh,
And welcomes in the morning sky.

Songs of birds begin their cheer,
Revealing magic drawing near.
With every note, the day is spun,
A tapestry where dreams run.

Glimmers dance on every leaf,
In silence found, we chase belief.
Hope entwined with every ray,
The mystique calls us into day.

## Beneath the Canopy of Enchantment

Beneath the leaves where shadows play,
A tapestry of green and gray.
The shimmering lights begin to weave,
A tale of magic we believe.

Mossy paths and hidden streams,
Guide us through enchanting dreams.
With every step, a soft refrain,
Calling forth the fey's domain.

Crickets chirp their mystic tune,
As twilight dances 'neath the moon.
The air is thick with whispered lore,
Each secret wrapped on nature's floor.

In this embrace of forest wide,
We find our spirit's gentle guide.
Underneath the ancient boughs,
The heart feels free, the soul allows.

## Twilight Tales in the Faerie Realm

In twilight's glow, the stories stir,
With whispers soft, the fey confer.
Each tale a spark in fading light,
A journey beyond the veil of night.

Fables spun of joy and woe,
With laughter echoing, soft and low.
Wings of gossamer brush the skies,
As magic in the darkness lies.

They gather round in circles bright,
To share their dreams, a wondrous sight.
With every laugh, the stars align,
In this realm where shadows shine.

The fey reveal their hidden ways,
In lingering twilight's gentle haze.
Through tales of wonder, we shall roam,
In faerie light, we find our home.

## Lanterns in the Woodland Night

In the dark where shadows creep,
Lanterns glow, their secrets keep.
Whispers deep in the quiet trees,
Carried softly on the breeze.

Stars above begin to shine,
Dancing lights, a grand design.
Echoes of the night unfold,
Tales of magic, softly told.

Moonlight filters through the leaves,
As the nightingale believes.
Every flicker, every sound,
Mysteries of the woods abound.

Footsteps wander, hearts collide,
Nature's beauty as our guide.
Together here, we find our peace,
Lanterns flicker, worries cease.

So let us wander hand in hand,
In this dreamlike, gentle land.
Beneath the stars, our spirits soar,
Lanterns in the night, evermore.

# Echoing Laughter in Enchanted Fields

Across the hills, where daisies sway,
Laughter dances through the day.
Echoes weave in the golden light,
Filling hearts with pure delight.

Children run with joyous screams,
Woven tight in sunny dreams.
Bees hum softly, butterflies play,
In the warmth of summer's ray.

Fields of green stretch wide and free,
Nature's playground, wild and glee.
Laughter rings, a sweet refrain,
In enchanted fields, we remain.

Fingers brush the gentle blooms,
In the air, a soft perfume.
With every laugh, the world awakes,
Joyful echoes, sweet heartaches.

As the sun begins to set,
Memories formed, we'll not forget.
Echoes fade but hearts will keep,
The laughter shared, the love vast and deep.

## The Glade Where Time Stands Still

In a glade where silence reigns,
Gentle whispers, soft refrains.
Time is but a fleeting dream,
Where shadows dance in silver gleam.

Mossy carpets, emerald hues,
Nature's symphony, gentle clues.
Here, worries seem to disappear,
As daylight fades, the night draws near.

Crystal streams flow through the trees,
Carried forth by the softest breeze.
Moments linger, softly drift,
In this glade, a precious gift.

With every heartbeat, still we stand,
In perfect peace, hand in hand.
Memories held in twilight's glow,
In the glade, love's whispers flow.

Moonlight casts a gentle glow,
Time dissolved in the night's flow.
In this place, we find our will,
Forever lost, yet always filled.

## Brushing Against Stardust Clouds

In the night where stardust plays,
Whispers echo in cosmic lays.
Brush of light on silken skies,
Dreams lift high and gently rise.

Galaxies swirl in a cosmic dance,
Where every star's a second chance.
Nebulas bloom with colors bright,
Filling hearts with pure delight.

Hands held high, we reach for more,
Brushing past the heavens' door.
Floating on a sea of dreams,
Life is more than what it seems.

Hope ignites in every spark,
Lighting paths in the vast dark.
Every glimmer tells a story,
In the night, we find the glory.

As dawn approaches, dreams will fade,
But in our hearts, the stardust stayed.
Forever timeless, this embrace,
Brushing against the cosmic grace.

9 781805 593805